For Maya Anne Materkole Pickersgill – my first great-niece

peace
Adrian Mitchell

Adrian Mitchell is a writer of poems, stories and plays for both adults and children. He started writing when he was nine and nobody has been able to stop him.

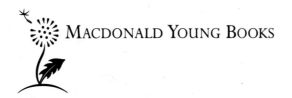

MACDONALD YOUNG BOOKS

Strawberry Drums

a book of poems with a beat
for you and all your friends to keep

put together by

ADRIAN MITCHELL

illustrated by Frances Lloyd

Illustrations copyright © Frances Lloyd 1989
This collection of poetry © Adrian Mitchell 1989

First published in Great Britain in 1989
by Macdonald Children's Books

Reprinted in 1990
by Simon & Schuster Young Books

Reprinted in 1998
by Macdonald Young Books
an imprint of Wayland Publishers Ltd
61 Western Road
Hove
East Sussex
BN3 1JD

Printed and bound in Belgium by Proost International Book Production

British Library Cataloguing in Publication Data available

ISBN: 0 7500 0364 2

Contents

WELCOME TO STRAWBERRY DRUMS

Poetry began in the times when everybody lived in tribes.
Some lived in caves, some lived in igloos, some lived in
huts on stilts or in smoky tents.
Some tribes were hunters, some tribes grew their food.
But every tribe made up poems.
And their poems were usually sung and danced.

Not long ago, people started to put poems in books.
But poems still want to be sung and danced.
I chose these poems because they are favourites of mine.
I also chose them because they are bright and sweet like strawberries.
And all of them have a beat – like drums.

Read them to yourself, shout them out loud, learn them by heart,
turn them into songs and dances and paintings.
Poems like to be used.
Don't bother if there's a line you don't understand.
Listen to the music of the poem.
Sooner or later the words will make sense, or, in some
cases, nonsense.

There's a Do It Yourself section to help you if you're
starting to write poems.
It's good to be able to write poems for your friends or
your parents or your dog's birthday.

Good luck with your writing and your reading and welcome
to the tribe that plays the Strawberry Drums.

Adrian Mitchell

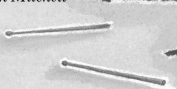

WHO IS DE GIRL?

who is de girl dat kick de ball
then jump for it over de wall

sallyann is a girl so full-o zest
sallyann is a girl dat just can't rest

who is de girl dat pull de hair
of de bully and make him scare

sallyann is a girl so full-o zest
sallyann is a girl dat just can't rest

who is de girl dat bruise she knee
when she fall from de mango tree

sallyann is a girl so full-o zest
sallyann is a girl dat just can't rest

who is de girl dat set de pace
when boys and girls dem start to race

sallyann is a girl so full-o zest
sallyann is a girl dat just can't rest

John Agard

RED BOOTS ON

Way down Geneva,
All along Vine,
Deeper than the snow drift
Love's eyes shine:

Mary Lou's walking
In the winter time.

She's got

Red boots on, she's got
Red boots on,
Kicking up the winter
Till the winter's gone.

So

Go by Ontario,
Look down Main,
If you can't find Mary Lou,
Come back again:

Sweet light burning
In winter's flame.

She's got

Snow in her eyes, got
A tingle in her toes
And new red boots on
Wherever she goes

So

All around Lake Street,
Up by St Paul,
Quicker than the white wind
Love takes all:

Mary Lou's walking
In the big snow fall.

She's got

Red boots on, she's got
Red boots on,
Kicking up the winter
Till the winter's gone.

Kit Wright

THE FLOWER-FED BUFFALOES

The flower-fed buffaloes of the spring
In the days of long ago,
Ranged where the locomotives sing
And the prairie flowers lie low:—
The tossing, blooming, perfumed grass
Is swept away by the wheat,
Wheels and wheels and wheels spin by
In the spring that still is sweet.
But the flower-fed buffaloes of the spring
Left us, long ago.
They gore no more, they bellow no more,
They trundle around the hills no more:-
With the Blackfeet, lying low,
With the Pawnees, lying low,
Lying low.

Vachel Lindsay

JABBERWOCKY

'Twas brillig, and the slithy toves
   Did gyre and gimble in the wabe;
All mimsy were the borogroves,
   And the mome raths outgrabe.

"Beware the Jabberwock, my son!
   The jaws that bite, the claws that catch!
Beware the Jubjub bird, and shun
   The frumious Bandersnatch!"

He took his vorpal sword in hand:
   Long time the manxome foe he sought –
So rested he by the Tumtum tree,
   And stood awhile in thought.

And as in uffish thought he stood,
   The Jabberwock, with eyes of flame,
Came whiffling through the tulgey wood,
   And burbled as it came!

One, two! One, two! And through and through
   The vorpal blade went snicker-snack!
He left it dead, and with its head
   He went galumphing back.

"And hast thou slain the Jabberwock!
   Come to my arms, my beamish boy!
O frabjous day! Callooh! Callay!"
   He chortled in his joy.

'Twas brillig, and the slithy toves
   Did gyre and gimble in the wabe;
All mimsy were the borogroves,
   And the mome raths outgrabe.

Lewis Carroll

Scorflufus

(By a well-known National Health Victim No. 3908631)

There are many diseases,
That strike people's kneeses,
Scorflufus! is one by name
It comes from the East
Packed in bladders of yeast
So the Chinese must take half the blame.

There's a case in the files
Of Sir Barrington-Pyles
While hunting a fox one day
Shot up in the air
And *remained hanging there!*
While the hairs on his socks turned grey.

Aye! Scorflufus had struck
At man, beast and duck!
And the knees of the world went Bong!
Some knees went Ping!
Other knees turned to string
From Balham to old Hong-Kong.

Should you hold your life dear,
Then the remedy's clear,
If you're offered some yeast – don't eat it!
Turn the offer down flat –
Don your travelling hat –
Put an egg in your boot – and beat it!

Spike Milligan

WHAT'S IN THERE?

What's in there?
Gold and money.
Where's my share?
The mousie's run away with it.
Where's the mousie?
In her housie?
Where's her housie?
In the wood.
Where's the wood?
Fire burnt it.
Where's the fire?
Water quenched it.
Where's the water?
Brown bull drank it.
Where's the brown bull?
Behind Burnie's hill.
Where's Burnie's hill?
All dressed in snow.
Where's the snow?
Sun melted it.
Where's the sun?
High, high up in the air.

Anonymous

THE MAN OF DOUBLE DEED

There was a man of double deed
Sowed his garden full of seed.
When the seed began to grow,
'Twas like a garden full of snow;
When the snow began to melt,
'Twas like a ship without a belt;
When the ship began to sail,
'Twas like a bird without a tail;
When the bird began to fly,
'Twas like an eagle in the sky;
When the sky began to roar,
'Twas like a lion at the door;
When the door began to crack,
'Twas like a stick across my back;
When my back began to smart,
'Twas like a penknife in my heart;
When my heart began to bleed,
'Twas death and death and death indeed.

Anonymous

THE TYGER

Tyger! Tyger! burning bright
In the forests of the night,
What immortal hand or eye
Could frame thy fearful symmetry?

In what distant deeps or skies
Burned the fire of thine eyes?
On what wings dare he aspire?
What the hand dare seize the fire?

And what shoulder, and what art,
Could twist the sinews of thy heart?
And when thy heart began to beat,
What dread hand? And what dread feet?

What the hammer? What the chain?
In what furnace was thy brain?
What the anvil? What dread grasp
Dare its deadly terrors clasp?

When the stars threw down their spears
And watered heaven with their tears,
Did he smile his work to see?
Did he who made the Lamb make thee?

Tyger! Tyger! burning bright
In the forests of the night,
What immortal hand or eye
Dare frame thy fearful symmetry?

William Blake

THE TIGER

The tiger roars at the end of the point.
What does he want? He wants to eat,
Eat wildfowl, eat wild pig,
Eat sambur-deer, eat chevrotin,
The striped tiger that crosses the sea –
Do not forget this in the telling.
The headlands are the land of the tiger.
The tiger has sworn an oath against someone,
The tiger jumps five fathoms,
Dodge the tiger, jump to the right.
The tiger walks the length of a tree-trunk,
The tiger sees a high hill,
The tiger sleeps at noonday.
Get up, O tiger, and walk the forest.
The tiger looks for live beasts,
The tiger walks to Mount Ophir,
That is the tiger's place of origin,
There is his second-chief, there is his grandfather.
There is his second-chief, there is his high-chief,
There lives the great-chief-of-tigers.
The tiger dies at the house of his great chief.

By the Jakun people of Malaysia

CHILD ON TOP OF A GREENHOUSE

The wind billowing out the seat of my britches,
My feet crackling splinters of glass and dried putty,
The half-grown chrysanthemums staring up like accusers,
Up through the streaked glass, flashing with sunlight,
A few white clouds all rushing eastward,
A line of elms plunging and tossing like horses,
And everyone, everyone pointing up and shouting!

Theodore Roethke

THE WONDERFUL CLOCK

I saw the clock in Wells
   Which an old monk made to chime,
With a doll to ring the bells
   And a star to tell the time,
With knights to tilt the hour
   From noon round to noon,
And the minutes in the power
   Of the sun and the moon.

Eleanor Farjeon

Names

They call you names for the fun of it,
To make your insides weak,
To injure all of your happiness
And tell you you're a SIKH.

To them you're totally different,
To them you're Lower Class,
They'll hit you and hurt you as much as they can
Till your insides are eaten at last.

They say that you're brown and they hate you,
And they never ever go away,
They've become a part of your life now,
And I fear that they're here to stay.

Kirandeep Chahal

LAST OF MY KIND

Was a giant
Not long ago,
Sat in wood,
Watched things grow.

Was the last
Of his kind,
Sat in wood,
Did not mind

When the rain
Fell on head,
When the fox
Shared his bed.

Not long ago
Was a witch.
Happy thing
Lived in ditch.

Was the last
Of her kind,
Wore old rags,
Did not mind.

Giant and witch
Sometimes talked,
In the wood
Sometimes walked.

Doctor came
Took witch away,
In a home
Had to stay.

Had not meant
To be unkind.
Said poor witch
Was out of mind.

She spoke of giant,
Spoke of fern,
To the ditch
Wished to return.

Pined and sighed,
Sad to say,
In a month
Passed away.

Though giant kept
Out of sight
He tended ditch
Day and night.

He lived a year,
Lived a day,
Then giant too
Pined away.

All this happened
I might say
Mile or so
From motorway.

In the forest
I sometimes walk,
With giant's ghost
Sometimes talk.

He tells me all
This is true,
Now I'm telling
Back to you.

I believe,
For you see,
I believe
Witch ordinary.

And the giant,
That he too
Was human as
You and you.

Giant was simple
As a babe,
Witch's mind
Like a cave,

And both lived
A different way
To what's expected
Now today.

I too live
In the wood,
Live on leaves
And rabbits' blood.

Munch the leaves,
Read the stars,
From hidey-hole
Watch the cars.

Am the last
Of my kind,
Do not wish
To be defined.

Brian Patten

THE JUMBLIES

They went to sea in a Sieve, they did,
  In a Sieve they went to sea:
In spite of all their friends could say,
On a winter's morn, on a stormy day,
  In a Sieve they went to sea!
And when the Sieve turned round and round,
And every one cried, "You'll all be drowned!"
They called aloud, "Our Sieve ain't big,
But we don't care a button! we don't care a fig!
  In a Sieve we'll go to sea!"
  Far and few, far and few,
    Are the lands where the Jumblies live;
  Their heads are green, and their hands are blue,
    And they went to sea in a Sieve.

They sailed away in a Sieve, they did,
  In a Sieve they sailed so fast,
With only a beautiful pea-green veil
Tied with a riband by way of a sail,
  To a small tobacco-pipe mast;
And every one said, who saw them go,
"O won't they be soon upset, you know!
For the sky is dark, and the voyage is long,
And happen what may, it's extremely wrong
  In a Sieve to sail so fast!"
  Far and few, far and few,
    Are the lands where the Jumblies live;
  Their heads are green, and their hands are blue,
    And they went to sea in a Sieve.

The water it soon came in, it did,
    The water it soon came in;
So to keep them dry, they wrapped their feet
In a pinky paper all folded neat,
    And they fastened it down with a pin.
And they passed the night in a crockery-jar,
And each of them said, "How wise we are!
Though the sky be dark, and the voyage be long,
Yet we never can think we were rash or wrong,
    While round in our Sieve we spin!"
    Far and few, far and few,
      Are the lands where the Jumblies live:
    Their heads are green, and their hands are blue,
      And they went to sea in a Sieve.

And all night long they sailed away;
    And when the sun went down,
They whistled and warbled a moony song
To the echoing sound of a coppery gong,
    In the shade of the mountains brown.
"O Timballo! How happy we are,
When we live in a sieve and a crockery-jar,
And all night long in the moonlight pale,
We sail away with a pea-green sail,
    In the shade of the mountains brown!"
    Far and few, far and few,
      Are the lands where the Jumblies live;
    Their heads are green, and their hands are blue,
      And they went to sea in a Sieve.

They sailed to the Western Sea, they did,
　To a land all covered with trees,
And they bought an Owl, and a useful Cart,
And a pound of Rice, and a Cranberry Tart,
　And a hive of silvery Bees.
And they bought a Pig, and some green Jack-daws,
And a lovely Monkey with lollipop paws,
And forty bottles of Ring-Bo-Ree,
　And no end of Stilton Cheese.
　Far and few, far and few,
　　Are the lands where the Jumblies live;
　Their heads are green, and their hands are blue,
　　And they went to sea in a Sieve.

And in twenty years they all came back,
　In twenty years or more,
And every one said, "How tall they've grown!
For they've been to the Lakes, and the Torrible Zone,
　And the hills of the Chankly Bore;"
And they drank their health, and gave them a feast
Of dumplings made of beautiful yeast;
And every one said, "If we only live,
We too will go to sea in a Sieve, –
　To the hills of the Chankly Bore!"
　Far and few, far and few,
　　Are the lands where the Jumblies live;
　Their heads are green, and their hands are blue,
　　And they went to sea in a Sieve.

Edward Lear

HUNDREDS AND THOUSANDS

The sound of hounds
on red sand thundering

Hundreds and thousands
of mouths glistening

The blood quickening
Thunder and lightning

The hunted in dread
of the hundreds running

The sound of thunder
A white moon reddening

Thousands of mad hounds
on red sand marauding

Thundering onwards
in hundreds and thundreds

Thundreds and thundreds
Thundering   Thundering

Roger McGough

THE BEST BEAST OF THE FAT-STOCK SHOW AT EARLS COURT

(in monosyllables)

The Best Beast of the Show
Is fat,
He goes by the lift –
They all do that.

This lift, large as a room,
(Yet the beasts bunch),
Goes up with a groan,
They have not oiled the winch.

Not yet to the lift
Goes the Best Beast,
He has to walk on the floor to make a show
First.

Great are his horns,
Long his fur,
The Beast came from the North
To walk here.

Is he not fat?
Is he not fit?
Now in a crown he walks
To the lift.

When he lay in his pen,
In the close heat,
His head lolled, his eyes
Were not shut for sleep.

Slam the lift door,
Push it up with a groan,
Will they kill the Beast now?
Where has he gone?

When he lay in the straw
His heart beat so fast
His sides heaved, I touched his side
As I walked past.

I touched his side,
I touched the root of his horns;
The breath of the Beast
Came in low moans.

Stevie Smith

Backwater Blues

When it rains five days and the skies turn dark as night
When it rains five days and the skies turn dark as night
Then trouble's takin' place in the lowlands at night

I woke up this mornin', can't even get out of my door
I woke up this mornin', can't even get out of my door
That's enough trouble to make a poor girl wonder where she want to go

Then they rowed a little boat about five miles 'cross the farm
Then they rowed a little boat about five miles 'cross the farm
I packed all my clothes, throwed them in and they rowed me along

When it thunders and lightnin' and the wind begins to blow
When it thunders and lightnin' and the wind begins to blow
There's thousands of people ain't got no place to go

Then I went and stood upon some high old lonesome hill
Then I went and stood upon some high old lonesome hill
Then looked down on the house where I used to live

Back-water blues done caused me to pack my things and go
Back-water blues done caused me to pack my things and go
'Cause my house fell down and I can't live there no more

Oh – I can't move no more
Oh – I can't move no more
There ain't no place for a poor old girl to go

Bessie Smith

YELLOW SUBMARINE

In the town where I was born
lived a man who sailed the sea,
and he told us of his life,
in the land of submarines.
So we sailed on to the sun,
till we found the sea of green,
and we lived beneath the waves,
 in our yellow submarine.

We all live in a yellow submarine,
yellow submarine, yellow submarine,
we all live in a yellow submarine,
yellow submarine, yellow submarine.

And our friends are all aboard,
many more of them live next door,
and the band begins to play.

We all live in a yellow submarine,
yellow submarine, yellow submarine,
we all live in a yellow submarine,
yellow submarine, yellow submarine.

As we live a life of ease,
everyone of us has all we need,
sky of blue and sea of green,
in our yellow submarine.

We all live in a yellow submarine,
yellow submarine, yellow submarine,
we all live in a yellow submarine,
yellow submarine, yellow submarine.

John Lennon and Paul McCartney

THE RED WHEELBARROW

so much depends
upon

a red wheel
barrow

glazed with rain
water

beside the white
chickens

William Carlos Williams

TOAD

Stop looking like a purse. How could a purse
squeeze under the rickety door and sit,
full of satisfaction, in a man's house?

You clamber towards me on your four corners —
one hand, one foot, one hand, one foot.

I love you for being a toad,
for crawling like a Japanese wrestler,
and for not being frightened.

I put you in my purse hand, not shutting it,
and set you down outside directly under
every star.

A jewel in your head? Toad,
you've put one in mine,
a tiny radiance in a dark place.

Norman MacCaig

DO IT YOURSELF

When you've heard some of these poems read aloud you may
like to make your own. One of the best ways to
start making poems is by copying poems you like.
Here's a famous poem which lots of people have made their own.

Down behind the dustbin
I met a dog called Jim.
He didn't know me
And I didn't know him.

Michael Rosen

I've done lots of versions of that, but the one most people like
is this:

Down behind the dustbin
I met a pup called Chappie
I said What's the matter?
He said I wet me nappie.

Now you try it.

Down behind the dustbin
I met a dog called Jack
....
....

All sorts of things could happen to Jack. He could hurt his back, or
eat a mack, or paint his tail black. It's up to you.

Now you invent your own dog.

Down behind the dustbin
I met a dog called ....
....
....

Some time ago I wrote a poem with the chorus "I like that stuff". Lots of people found it fun to copy, including Roger McGough, who wrote a poem "I hate that stuff" which was the opposite of mine. Here's my one.

STUFFERATION

Lovers lie around in it
Broken glass is found in it
Grass
I like that stuff

Tuna fish get trapped in it
Legs come wrapped in it
Nylon
I like that stuff

Eskimos and tramps chew it
Madame Tussaud gave status to it
Wax
I like that stuff

Elephants get sprayed with it
Scotch is made with it
Water
I like that stuff

Clergy are dumbfounded by it
Bones are surrounded by it
Flesh
I like that stuff

Harps are strung with it
Mattresses are sprung with it
Wire
I like that stuff

Carpenters make cots of it
Undertakers use lots of it
Wood
I like that stuff

Cigarettes are lit by it
Pensioners get happy when they sit by it
Fire
I like that stuff

Dankworth's alto is made of it, most of it,
Scoobdidoo is composed of it
Plastic
I like that stuff

Apemen take it to make them hairier
I ate a ton of it in Bulgaria
Yoghurt
I like that stuff

Man-made fibres and raw materials
Old rolled gold and breakfast cereals
Platinum linoleum
I like that stuff

Skin on my hands
Hair on my head
Toenails on my feet
And linen on the bed

Well I like that stuff
Yes I like that stuff
The earth
Is made of earth
And I like that stuff

Adrian Mitchell

Now it's your turn. Hang on, before you start, here's a secret:

>   Use your feet
>   To find the beat.

That means, why not tap out the rhythm of the poem you're writing?
Better still, get up and walk around to the rhythm of the poem
while you're making it. It works for me and it might for you.
Go ahead.

The first two lines of each verse –

Harps are strung with it
Mattresses are sprung with it –
are a kind of a riddle.
The answer to the riddle is the next line –
Wire –
And the last line is the chorus –
I like that stuff, or, I hate that stuff.

The first two lines can have a rhyme, like strung and sprung
or trapped and wrapped, but if you don't feel like
using rhymes, that's OK by me.
You could start by making a list of things you like or things
you hate. And see where you go from there. Good luck!

BLUE TOBOGGANS

scarves for the apaches
wet gloves for snowballs
whoops for white clouds
and blue toboggans

stamping for a tingle
lamps for four o'clock
steamed glass for buses
and blue toboggans

tuning-forks for Wenceslas
white fogs for Prestwick
mince pies for the Eventides
and blue toboggans

TV for the lonely
a long haul for heaven
a shilling for the gas
and blue toboggans

Edwin Morgan

ALLIE

Allie, call the birds in,
  The birds from the sky!
Allie calls, Allie sings,
  Down they all fly:
First there came
Two white doves,
  Then a sparrow from his nest,
Then a clucking bantam hen,
  Then a robin red-breast.

Allie, call the beasts in,
  The beasts, every one!
Allie calls, Allie sings,
  In they run:
First there came
Two black lambs,
  Then a grunting Berkshire sow,
Then a dog without a tail,
  Then a red and white cow.

Allie, call the fish up,
  The fish from the stream!
Allie calls, Allie sings,
  Up they all swim:
First there came
Two gold fish,
  A minnow and a miller's thumb,
Then a school of little trout,
  Then the twisting eels come.

Allie, call the children,
  Call them from the green!
Allie calls, Allie sings,
  Soon they run in:
First there came
Tom and Madge,
  Kate and I who'll not forget
How we played by the water's edge
  Till the April sun set.

Robert Graves

What a Day it's Been!

Dear children, what a day it's been!
The kind of day when days
Are not what they are meant to be
In several kind of ways.

My eyes are dim for I have sobbed
Twelve tears of Platform Brine,
There'll *never* be another Niece
As innocent as mine!

Mine was the One! Mine was the Two;
Mine was the Three and Four,
And I have heard her parents say
She rose to Seven or more!

So be it. She is gone, and I
Am left at Waterloo;
Half magical, half tragical,
And, half-an-hour . . . or two.

Mervyn Peake

And God Said to the Little Boy

And God said to the little boy
As the little boy came out of chapel
Little boy, little boy, little boy
Did you eat that there apple?
And the little boy answered No, Lord.

And God said to the little girl
As the little girl came out of chapel
Little girl, little girl, little girl,
Did you eat that there apple?
And the little girl answered No, Lord.

Then the Lord pointed with his finger
And fixed them both with his stare,
And he said in a voice like a Rolls Royce
Well, what are them two cores doing there?

George Barker

LULLABY

It's my fat baby
I feel in my hood,
Oh, how heavy he is!
Ya ya! Ya ya!

When I turn my head
He smiles at me, my baby,
Hidden deep in my hood,
Oh, how heavy he is!
Ya ya! Ya ya!

How pretty he is when he smiles
With his two teeth, like a little walrus!
Oh, I'd rather my baby were heavy,
So long as my hood is full!

*Song of the Eskimo people
of Greenland*

SILVER

Slowly, silently, now the moon
Walks the night in her silver shoon;
This way, and that, she peers, and sees
Silver fruit upon silver trees;
One by one the casements catch
Her beams beneath the silvery thatch;
Couched in his kennel, like a log,
With paws of silver sleeps the dog;
From their shadowy cote the white breasts peep
Of doves in silver-feathered sleep;
A harvest mouse goes scampering by,
With silver claws, and silver eye;
And moveless fish in the water gleam,
By silver reeds in a silver stream.

Walter de la Mare

BLOW THE STARS HOME

Blow the Stars home, Wind, blow the Stars home
Ere Morning drowns them in golden foam.

Eleanor Farjeon

NIGHT WAY

In beauty	may I walk
All day long	may I walk
Through the returning seasons	may I walk
Beautifully will I possess again	
Beautifully birds	
Beautifully joyful birds	
On the trail marked with pollen	may I walk
With grasshoppers about my feet	may I walk
With dew about my feet	may I walk
With beauty	may I walk
With beauty before me	may I walk
With beauty behind me	may I walk
With beauty above me	may I walk
With beauty all around me	may I walk
In old age, wandering on a trail of beauty, lively,	may I walk
In old age, wandering on a trail of beauty, living again,	may I walk
It is finished in beauty	
It is finished in beauty	

From the Navajo Night Way ceremony

ACKNOWLEDGEMENTS

The Publishers wish to thank all the authors and publishers who have given permission for copyright material to be used in this anthology.

'Who is de Girl' copyright © John Agard.

'Red Boots On' copyright © Kit Wright.

Spike Milligan and W.H. Allen & Co. Plc for 'Scorflufus' from *A Dustbin of Milligan* (Tandem Books).

William Collins & Co. (1926) for 'The Wonderful Clock' and 'Blow the Stars Home' from *Joan's Door* by Eleanor Farjeon.

'Child on Top of a Greenhouse' by Theodore Roethke copyright © 1946 by Editorial Publications Inc. From *The Collected Poems of Theodore Roethke* reprinted by permission of Doubleday, a division of Bantam, Doubleday, Dell, Publishing Group, Inc. (USA & Canada), and Faber and Faber Ltd © Theodore Roethke 1948 (UK and Commonwealth).

Kirandeep Chahal for 'Names' from the Hillingdon NAPE Journal Spring 1985.

'Last of My Kind' by Brian Patten from *Gargling With Jelly* (Kestrel Books), © Brian Patten 1985, reproduced by permission of Penguin Books Ltd and Anthony Sheil Associates.

'Hundreds and Thousands' copyright © Roger McGough from *Nailing the Shadow* (Viking Kestrel 1987), reprinted by permission of the Peters Fraser & Dunlop Group Ltd.

The Executor James MacGibbon and *The Collected Poems of Stevie Smith* (Penguin Modern Classics) for 'The Best Beast of the Fat-Stock Show at Earls Court'. US rights: Stevie Smith: *The Collected Poems* copyright © 1937, 1938, 1950, 1957, 1966, 1971, 1972 by Stevie Smith. Reprinted by permission of New Directions Publishing Corporation.

'Backwater Blues' by Bessi Smith © 1927, 1974 FRANK MUSIC CORP. © Renewed 1955 FRANK MUSIC CORP. International Copyright Secured. All Rights Reserved. Used by Permission.

'Yellow Submarine' © 1966 Northern Songs, under licence to SBK Songs Ltd., 3–5 Rathbone Place, London W1P 1DA.

'The Red Wheelbarrow' William Carlos Williams: *Collected Poems 1909–1939, Vol. I.* Copyright © 1938 by New Directions Publishing Corporation. Reprinted by permission of New Directions Publishing Corporation. U.S. and Canadian rights only. UK and Commonwealth rights Carcanet Press Ltd.

Norman MacCaig and Chatto & Windus for 'Toad' from *The Equal Skies* by Norman MacCaig.

Michael Rosen and André Deutsch Ltd for 'Down Behind the Dustbin' from *Mind Your Own Business*, 1974.

Adrian Mitchell and W.H. Allen & Co. Plc for 'Stufferation' from *Nothingmas Day* (Allison & Busby).

Edwin Morgan and Carcanet Press Ltd for 'Blue Toboggans' from *Poems of Thirty Years*, 1982.

'Allie' from *Collected Poems* 1975 by Robert Graves. Copyright © 1975 by Robert Graves, by permission of AP Watt Limited on behalf of The Executors of The Estate of Robert Graves.
US rights: reprinted by permission of Oxford University Press, Inc. New York.

Mervyn Peake and Methuen Children's Books for 'What a Day it's Been' from *Rhymes Without Reason*.

'And God Said to the Little Boy' reprinted by permission of Faber and Faber Ltd from *To Aylsham Fair* by George Barker copyright © George Barker 1970.

The Literary Trustees of Walter de la Mare and The Society of Authors as their representative for 'Silver' from *Poems of Childhood* (Constable).

Every effort has been made to trace and contact copyright holders. The publishers will be pleased to make any necessary corrections in future printings, in the event of an error or omission in the use of copyright material.